Shall We Dance?

BALLROOM DANCE

by Wendy Hinote Lanier

FOCUS READERS

FOCUS READERS

www.focusreaders.com

Focus Readers is distributed by North Star Editions: sales@northstareditions.com | 888-417-0195

Produced for Focus Readers by Red Line Editorial.

Photographs ©: Tyler Olson/Shutterstock Images, cover, 1; MarkoNovkov/iStockphoto, 4–5; Library of Congress, 7; Tyler Olson/Shutterstock Images, 8; A_Lesik/Shutterstock Images, 10–11; Africa Studio/Shutterstock Images, 12; Igor Groshev/iStockphoto, 14–15; Anton Gvozdikov/Shutterstock Images, 17; David Haykazyan/Shutterstock Images, 18; Dmitry Morgan/Shutterstock Images, 20– 21, 29; AP Images, 22–23; Manvmedia/Shutterstock Images, 25; Wedding Stock Photo/Shutterstock Images, 27

ISBN
978-1-63517-272-0 (hardcover)
978-1-63517-337-6 (paperback)
978-1-63517-467-0 (ebook pdf)
978-1-63517-402-1 (hosted ebook)

Library of Congress Control Number: 2017935121

Printed in the United States of America
Mankato, MN
June, 2017

About the Author

Wendy Hinote Lanier is a native Texan and former elementary teacher who writes and speaks for children and adults on a variety of topics. She is the author of more than 20 books for children and young people. Some of her favorite people are dogs.

TABLE OF CONTENTS

CHAPTER 1

What Is Ballroom Dancing? 5

CHAPTER 2

What to Wear 11

CHAPTER 3

Basic Moves 15

TRY IT OUT

Box Step 20

CHAPTER 4

On with the Show! 23

Focus on Ballroom Dancing • 28

Glossary • 30

To Learn More • 31

Index • 32

WHAT IS BALLROOM DANCING?

Most fairy tales have happy endings. And somewhere in the story, there is usually a **ball**. The princess dances with her Prince Charming. They twirl and glide across the floor.

 A couple performs the tango.

But ballroom dancing isn't just for princes and princesses. You can ballroom dance, too.

Ballroom dancing has been around for centuries. It is also called social dancing. The original ballroom dances were held in the royal courts of Europe. These were complicated dances. They required a stiff **posture** and a variety of foot positions.

During the 1700s, a new dance became popular. It was called

 An illustration shows ballroom dancers at an 1872 military ball in New York City.

the waltz. Before the waltz, ballroom dancing had been a group activity. But the waltz made it a couples' activity. Partners touched each other for the first time. The waltz was also easy to learn.

> Today ballroom dancing is common at gatherings such as weddings and parties.

By the 1900s, ballroom dancing had moved out of the royal courts. Ordinary people began dancing in restaurants and hotels. Dance halls became popular, too.

Ballroom dances include the waltz, polka, fox-trot, tango, and quickstep. The dances move in a counterclockwise direction around the dance floor. Ballroom dancing involves style and grace. This makes it a pleasure to watch.

DANCE TIP

Different ballroom dances have different steps. Lessons will help you learn the steps.

CHAPTER 2

WHAT TO WEAR

There are two kinds of ballroom dance clothes. One is for practice. The other is for show.

Practice clothes are **formfitting**. But they are also flexible. Dance clothes for show are different.

Ballroom dancers often wear fancy outfits.

They are more formal and elegant. Women usually wear long, flowing dresses. These gowns are often sparkly. Women also wear glamorous makeup. Men wear dark dress pants, a plain white dress shirt, and a tie. Sometimes men wear **tuxedos**.

Dancers must have good shoes. The shoes should be comfortable. They should provide support and protection. Of course, they should look good, too. Shoes for both men and women have a thin **suede** sole. This allows dancers to glide across the floor with the right grip.

DANCE TIP

Heel protectors provide a strong grip. They help dance shoes last longer.

CHAPTER 3

BASIC MOVES

Most ballroom dances start from a closed position. This is when partners stand facing each other. The woman stands slightly to the man's right. She rests her left hand on the man's right shoulder.

Dancers perform in the closed position.

The man's right hand is placed on the woman's back. It goes just above her waist. He extends his left arm out. The woman places her right hand between his thumb and index finger.

The closed position allows the man to be the leader of the dance. The woman follows his lead.

DANCE TIP

Padded inserts for your shoes add comfort. They allow you to dance longer.

 The man is typically the leader in ballroom dancing.

He guides the couple around the dance floor. She responds to his movements. But the leader must also watch other couples. If he is not careful, the couples could bump into each other.

 Dancers perform the tango in a town square.

The dance steps depend on the music. Waltz, polka, fox-trot, tango, and quickstep all have different step **sequences**. Most people begin by learning the waltz.

BOX STEP

The basic step for the waltz is a box step. Each dancer completes a forward half box and a backward half box. A half box has three steps. The man typically starts by stepping forward.

1. Step forward with your left foot.
2. Step your right foot forward and to the side.
3. Bring your left foot together with your right foot.

Note that when dancing with a partner, the women's steps are reversed. She begins by stepping backward with her right foot.

Dancers perform the waltz.

CHAPTER 4

ON WITH THE SHOW!

In the early 1900s, ballroom dancing became a popular form of entertainment. Fred Astaire and Ginger Rogers were famous dancers. They performed in films during the 1930s and 1940s.

▷ **Fred Astaire and Ginger Rogers in 1935**

Everyone wanted to dance just like them. People tried to copy their dance style. Some danced at home. Soon people were entering dance contests and **marathons**.

Competitive ballroom dancing became popular in the late 1900s. It is sometimes called DanceSport. There are two main styles. One is called international style. It allows only closed position dancing. There is also American style. It uses the same steps as international.

 Dancers compete in a ballroom dancing competition.

But it allows open and separated dance moves, too. Competitions feature a variety of age ranges and ability levels.

DANCE TIP

The key to competitive dancing is to look happy and relaxed. If you are unsure of a step, the best approach is to fake it with confidence.

Ballroom dancing has become part of American **culture**. There are many places you can enjoy dancing. They include weddings and dance **studios**. Dance competitions continue to grow more popular, too. If you like to compete, you may

 A newlywed couple enjoys their first dance.

find DanceSport is right for you. No matter how you participate, you are likely to find ballroom dancing is lots of fun.

BALLROOM DANCING

Write your answers on a separate piece of paper.

1. Write a letter to a friend explaining the main idea of Chapter 1.

2. Do you think ballroom dancing would be hard to do? Why or why not?

3. Which dance changed ballroom dancing from a group activity to couples dancing ?
   - **A.** fox-trot
   - **B.** waltz
   - **C.** tango

4. How has ballroom dancing changed over the years?
   - **A.** Ballroom dancing is no longer popular.
   - **B.** Dancers now move in a clockwise direction.
   - **C.** Ballroom dancing is now popular beyond the royal courts.

5. What does **responds** mean in this book?

He guides the couple around the dance floor.
*She **responds** to his movements.*

   A. looks around

   B. reacts

   C. speaks

6. What does **elegant** mean in this book?

Dance clothes for show are different. They are
*more formal and **elegant**. Women usually wear*
long, flowing dresses.

   A. beautiful

   B. heavy

   C. flexible

Answer key on page 32.

GLOSSARY

ball
A formal party where people often dance.

culture
The way a group of people live; their customs, beliefs, and laws.

formfitting
Snug to one's body.

marathons
Dance contests to see who can dance the longest.

posture
The way a person holds or carries his or her body.

sequences
Orders of dance steps.

studios
Rooms or buildings where dancers practice.

suede
Leather with a soft texture.

tuxedos
Suits that men usually wear for formal occasions.

TO LEARN MORE

BOOKS

Hamilton, Sue H. *Ballroom*. Edina, MN: Abdo Publishing, 2011.

Royston, Angela. *Ballroom*. Chicago: Heinemann Library, 2013.

Thomas, Isabel. *Latin Dance*. Minneapolis: Lerner Publications, 2012.

NOTE TO EDUCATORS

Visit **www.focusreaders.com** to find lesson plans, activities, links, and other resources related to this title.

INDEX

A
American style, 24–25
Astaire, Fred, 23–24

B
box step, 20

C
closed position, 15–16, 24
clothes, 11–12
competitive dancing, 24–25, 26

D
DanceSport, 24, 26

E
Europe, 6

F
fox-trot, 9, 19

I
international style, 24

P
polka, 9, 19

Q
quickstep, 9, 19

R
Rogers, Ginger, 23–24
royal courts, 6, 8

S
shoes, 13, 16

T
tango, 9, 19

W
waltz, 7, 9, 19, 20